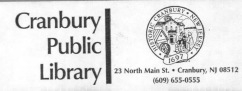

MOTHS

NICOLE HELGET

Published by Creative Education

P.O. Box 227, Mankato, Minnesota 56002

Creative Education is an imprint of The Creative Company

Design and production by Stephanie Blumenthal

Printed in the United States of America

Photographs by Alamy Images (blickwinkel), Entomological Society of America / Ries Memorial Slide Collection, Getty Images (National Geographic, Photonica), William T. Hark, Dave Leatherman

Library of Congress Cataloging-in-Publication Data

Helget, Nicole Lea, 1976–
Moths / by Nicole Helget.
p. cm. — (BugBooks)
Includes index.
ISBN-13: 978-1-58341-543-6
1. Moths—Juvenile literature. I. Title.

QL544.2.H46 2007
595.78—dc22   2006018245

First Edition
2 4 6 8 9 7 5 3 1

Moths dart under a streetlight.

They flutter their wings. They bump against the light. They are looking for other moths. Soon they will find a place to lay eggs.

MOTHS ARE INSECTS. A MOTH

 HAS TWO EYES AND

TWO FEELERS. THE

EYES WATCH FOR PRED-

ATORS SUCH AS BATS AND OTHER IN-

SECTS. THE FEELERS ARE CALLED

ANTENNAE (AN-TEN-NAY). THEY

ARE USED TO SMELL. SOME MOTHS

HAVE A LONG TONGUE. THEY USE IT

TO SUCK UP NECTAR.

Some moths' antennae look like feathers.

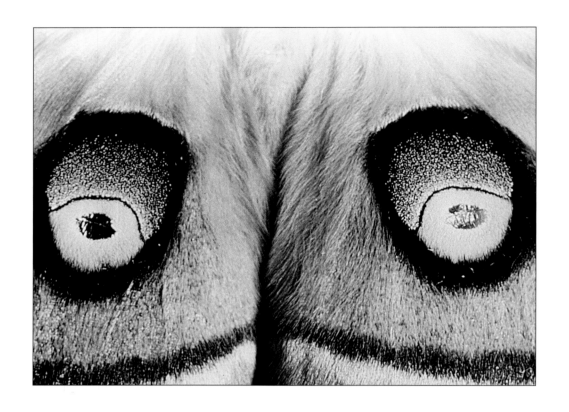

TRICKY MOTHS Some moths have spots on their wings. The spots look like big eyes. They scare away predators. Other moths look like tree bark. This helps them hide.

Moths' wings have different shapes.

Moths have wings and six legs. The wings are used to fly. They have tiny, colorful scales on them. A moth's legs have ORGANS on the end of them. The organs help the moth taste things. A moth breathes through its belly. The belly has tiny air holes in it.

FEMALE MOTHS CAN LAY 1,000
EGGS AT A TIME.

THEY LAY THEM ON
PLANTS. THE EGGS
ARE TINY. CATER-
PILLARS HATCH FROM THE EGGS.

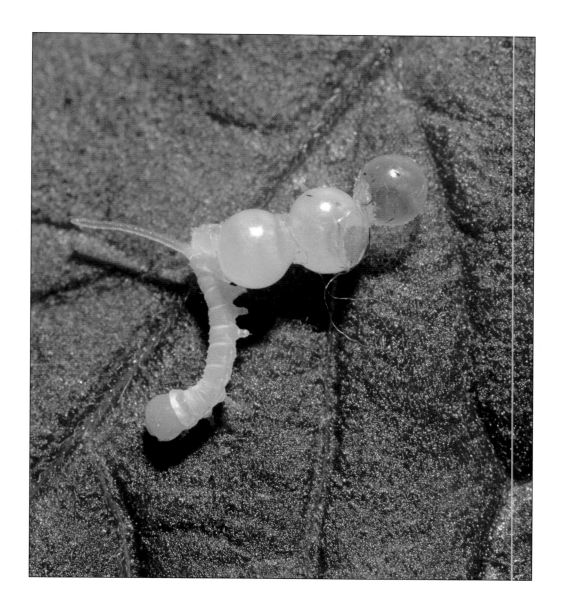

Caterpillars are small when they hatch.

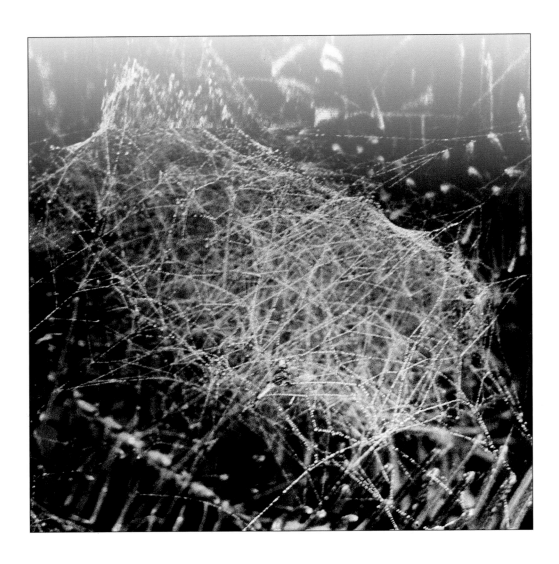

A cocoon keeps caterpillars safe.

A CATERPILLAR LOOKS AND MOVES

 LIKE A WORM.

IT EATS LOTS

OF PLANTS AND

GROWS FAST.

AFTER A WHILE,

THE CATERPILLAR SPINS A COCOON

AROUND ITSELF.

INSIDE THE COCOON, THE CATER-

PILLAR CHANGES

INTO A MOTH.

THE MOTH THEN

BREAKS OUT OF THE COCOON.

ADULT MOTHS LIVE ONLY A FEW

DAYS OR WEEKS.

Moths stretch their new wings.

BUTTERFLIES AND MOTHS *Butterflies and moths look alike. But they are different. Moths usually come out at night. Butterflies like daylight. Butterflies have lumps on the end of their antennae. Moths do not.*

MOTHS LIVE EVERYWHERE EX-
CEPT IN OCEANS. THEY LIKE WARM

PLACES BEST, SUCH
AS HAWAII AND
AUSTRALIA. IT IS
EASIER FOR MOTHS

TO FLY AND FIND FOOD THERE.

Moths like to rest on plant leaves.

Moths help flowers to grow.

MOST MOTHS ARE HELPFUL TO
PEOPLE. SOME PEOPLE USE CATER-

 PILLAR COCOONS TO
MAKE SILK. SILK IS
MADE INTO CLOTHES.

MOTHS HELP FLOWERS GROW, TOO.
MOTHS FLY FROM FLOWER TO
FLOWER. THEY CARRY TINY PLANT
PARTS ON THEIR BODIES. THEY TAKE
IT TO OTHER FLOWERS.

SOME CATERPILLARS EAT FARM-
ERS' PLANTS. CATERPILLARS CAN ALSO

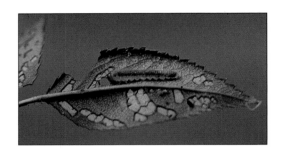

EAT CLOTHING.
SOME PEOPLE
PUT MOTHBALLS
IN THEIR CLOSETS. MOTHBALLS
SMELL BAD. THEY KEEP THE CATER-
PILLARS AWAY.

Plant-eating caterpillars become pretty moths.

The giant hercules (HER-KYOO-LEEZ) moth is the biggest moth. It is 12 inches (30.5 cm) across! The smallest moth is only as big as a baby's pinky fingernail!

CANNED MOTHS   In Africa, many people like to eat moth caterpillars. Some people put them in cans and sell them.

MOTHS ARE ALL AROUND US.
NEXT TIME YOU ARE UNDER A
STREETLIGHT AT NIGHT, LOOK UP.
LOTS OF MOTHS WILL BE FLUTTER-
ING AROUND!

Moths are most active at night.

GLOSSARY

COCOON — A LITTLE POUCH THAT HELPS A CATERPILLAR CHANGE INTO A MOTH

INSECTS — BUGS THAT HAVE SIX LEGS

NECTAR — A SWEET LIQUID THAT PLANTS MAKE

ORGANS — SPECIAL PARTS INSIDE THE BODY OF AN ANIMAL OR PERSON

PREDATORS — ANIMALS THAT KILL AND EAT OTHER ANIMALS

INDEX

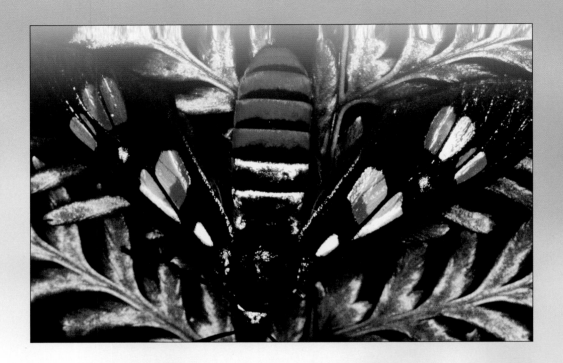